P9-DTA-005

DEDICATION

This book is dedicated to Barbara Kuroff, former editorial director of Writer's Digest Books and a friend to writers everywhere.
I first proposed three "little books" to Writer's Digest Books five years ago. Over time our vision for the books changed, as did market conditions and publishing priorities. Barb's faith in the project never wavered. Quite simply, were it not for her persistent advocacy, these volumes would not exist.

ACKNOWLEDGMENTS

Robin Estrin, for her constancy and encouragement.
Jane Friedman, who stuck her neck out in a new job to acquire this book.
Lavern Hall, who will always be my first publisher.
Lisa Kuhn and Grace Ring, who made this a beautiful book with their design.
Kirk Nesset, the best short fiction critiquer I have ever encountered.
Kelly Nickell, who made this a better book with her editing.
Rita Rosenkranz, who negotiated the contract and freed me to write.
Kathie Westerfield, who provided me with a writing haven when I most needed it.

TABLE OF CONTENTS

2/2010 For Lisa J.
from Grandma J

Writer's Little Instruction Book

INSPIRATION &
MOTIVATION

PAUL RAYMOND MARTIN

WRITER'S DIGEST BOOKS
Cincinnati, Ohio
www.writersdigest.com

Writer's Little Instruction Book: Inspiration & Motivation. © 2005 by Paul Raymond Martin. Manufactured in the United States of America. All rights reserved. No part of this book may be reproduced in any form or by any electronic or mechanical means including information storage and retrieval systems without permission in writing from the publisher, except by a reviewer, who may quote brief passages in a review. Published by Writer's Digest Books, an imprint of F+W Publications, Inc., 4700 East Galbraith Road, Cincinnati, OH 45236. (800) 289-0963. First edition.

Visit our Web site at www.writersdigest.com for information on more resources for writers. To receive a free weekly e-mail newsletter delivering tips and updates about writing and about Writer's Digest products, register directly at our Web site at http://newsletters.fwpublications.com.

09 08 07 06 05   5 4 3 2 1

Library of Congress Cataloging-in-Publication Data

Martin, Paul Raymond.
  Writer's little instruction book. Inspiration & motivation : includes more than 300 story starters and prompts / by Paul Raymond Martin.
    p. cm.
  ISBN 1-58297-342-3 (pbk. : alk. paper)
  1. Authorship–Psychological aspects. 2. Authorship. I. Title: Inspiration & motivation. II. Title.
  PN171.P83M37 2005   2004028834
  808'.02—dc22

Edited by Kelly Nickell
Designed by Lisa Buchanan-Kuhn and Grace Ring
Cover Photography by Al Parrish
Page Layout by Grace Ring
Production Coordinated by Robin Richie

F+W PUBLICATIONS, INC.

INTRODUCTION:
INSPIRATION & MOTIVATION

The response to *The Writer's Little Instruction Book: 385 Secrets for Writing Well & Getting Published*, originally released in 1998, was both gratifying and surprising. My little book, adopted by classroom teachers from middle school through college, also became a hit at writers' workshops. While I didn't anticipate so many readers would draw life lessons from it, as well as inspiration and instruction for their writing, the results have been most rewarding. Thus, my little book has grown into a series of three:

Writer's Little Instruction Book: Inspiration & Motivation
Writer's Little Instruction Book: Craft & Technique
Writer's Little Instruction Book: Getting Published

Each volume includes motivational quotes and secrets for effective writing from prominent authors and editors, original aphorisms to keep you focused and on track, anecdotes to illustrate key points related to writing and the writing life, and story starters or publishing strategies to inspire your work when you're stuck or when you just want to try something new.

May your stride be longer returning from the mailbox than on the way to it.

INSPIRATION:
You Gotta Keep
Your Saw in the Wood

If one waits for the right time to come before writing, **the right time never comes**.

—James Russell Lowell, poet and critic

Writing is finally a series of permissions you give yourself to be expressive in certain ways. To invent. To leap. To fly. To fall.

—Susan Sontag, author, essayist, and playwright

I'm only really alive when I'm writing.

—Tennessee Williams, Pulitzer Prize-winning playwright

You can't build a reputation on what you're going to do.

—Henry Ford, U.S. industrialist and pioneer automobile manufacturer

In writing, as in most endeavors, **sweat rules** over inspiration.

> It's been said that literature is a high form of gossip. Heard any good stuff lately? Do tell!

> To paraphrase Mark Twain, the man or woman who doesn't write holds no advantage over the one who can't.

> People who talk a lot say they could write a book if only they had the time. Writers are the ones who quit talking so much.

What some folks call **genius** is simply **intelligence** and **awareness** applied with discipline.

Write with major intent. Nothing less will do.

➤ Begin each day's writing with whatever you most want to write about.

➤ Trust yourself to generate new writing ideas tomorrow and the next day and the next.

➤ You cannot decide once and for all to be a writer. You must renew your commitment to writing every day.

See life as it is, but write about life as it might be.

Fear of failure, fear of success: If you give in to fear, **it's all the same.**

➤ You will never overcome your fear that your writing is insipid or incomprehensible or trivial—write in spite of the fear.

> The Internet offers a superhighway of information and opinion, even a sense of community. But writing remains a self-made path into the unknown.

Your writing must be as **honest** as your **courage** allows.

Good ideas aren't hard to come by. **Good writing** is.

In writing, as in most endeavors, there is **always room for excellence.**

➤ What other people say about your writing may affect your writing, but never your commitment to your writing.

➤ Writing is not about ideas, it is about the expression of ideas—a written expression.

SQUIGGLY MARKS ON A PIECE OF PAPER

A few years ago, I was sprawled on my couch reading "The Ledge," a story in Stephen King's *Night Shift*. In the story, a man afraid of heights has to step out onto the ledge of a skyscraper and make his way around it in order to re-enter the building. I became the man in the story. Goose bumps pebbled my arms. Shivers zipped up and down my spine. Sweat beaded on my forehead. All the while, I was perfectly safe on my couch. I kept reading. My chest tightened. My breathing shallowed. I kept reading.

It's amazing that, at a time and place wholly apart from the writing, at a time and a place wholly unknown to the writer, a bunch of squiggly marks on a piece of paper can evoke such a response from a reader.

It's amazing that, at a time and place wholly apart from your writing, at a time and place wholly apart from you, your words may move a some distant reader to feel something powerful, or to understand another person's actions.

A writer's gift is to exercise the imagination and conscience of others. What a miracle is this business of writing.

➤ Never use your writing as fodder for small talk.
It is more important than that and deserves better.

➤ Write less fiction of the mirror (looking inward)
and more fiction of the window (looking outward).

We write poorly in order
to learn to write well.

➤ Give yourself time to develop as a writer. Be patient with yourself.

Don't talk yourself **out of a story.** Instead, write the story **out of yourself.**

The road to unfinished work is paved with good intentions.

➤ If you came to writing later in life than most, glory in it. You have a perspective and appreciation of life unavailable to you earlier.

➤ You didn't start writing earlier because you weren't ready. You had other priorities and lessons to learn. Now, you are ready.

➤ Do not be concerned that the reader be moved by all your words, rather that the reader be moved by your words at all.

➤ Writing well is sometimes tedious. Having written well is always joyful.

The road to published work is always under construction.

The real voyage of discovery consists not in seeking **new land-scapes,** but in having **new eyes.**

—Marcel Proust, author of *Remembrance of Things Past*

The discipline of the written word punishes both stupidity and dishonesty.

—John Steinbeck, Pulitzer Prize-winning author of *The Grapes of Wrath*

For me, writing something down is the only road out.

—Anne Tyler, author of *Breathing Lessons*

I am to be allowed to write, and gradually return to the world.

—Virginia Woolf, author of *A Room of One's Own*

A writer's **reach for the stars** begins with a **reach for the keyboard.**

> You put words on paper. You teach, inform, motivate, entertain, evoke. The whole world envies you.

> You are a writer. You make squiggly marks on paper. People pay to look at them. Amazing.

➤ There is a direct correlation between the shine in your writing and the shine in the seat of your pants. In other words: sit and deliver.

➤ The harder one works at writing, the more often the muse visits.

Every word you write is a decision. The more decisions you make, the easier they become.

> In order for a writer's dream to become a reality, it must first be given up as a dream.

May your fingers **dance a glorious ensemble.**

You can't hurry excellence.

A tree gave its life that your
words might appear in print. May your
words be worthy of the tree.

➤ The limitations are few and the opportunities are
many, though we excuse ourselves by thinking just
the opposite.

➤ Write the book you would like to read. Start with
the scene where you would turn down the corner of
the page.

STORY STARTERS
Need some extra inspiration? Choose one of these story openings and run with it.

There were no witnesses to the death of Ivan Ilitch. No doubt he stepped back from the hickory as it fell. His hard hat probably saved him a concussion before the force of an adjacent hickory, long dead but pulled down by the tree Ivan felled, snapped his neck. There were no witnesses to the death of Ivan Ilitch. But Ivan was too smart to ever work the woods alone.

Is it possible to anger your guardian angel? His expression remained calm, but a quiver riffed across his wings. *Heaven forgive me, I hadn't meant to scream at my angel, Miguel.*

A few minutes after noon. No one in the restaurant is having bacon and eggs. Yet with every sip of coffee, I taste the bacon and eggs. Taste the memory of bacon and eggs. Taste the memory of Missy who served the bacon and eggs.

> If you aren't in the mood to write, writing will change your mood.

Writing **generates inspiration.** Not the other way around.

Twenty percent of a hummingbird's weight is **heart**. **Eighty** percent for a writer.

➤ As they say in competitive riding, "You must first throw your heart over the fence."

➤ Like the characters in *The Wizard of Oz*, you will find within yourself all you need to succeed as a writer.

The uphill stride is always shorter than the downhill stride.

➤ There are no shortcuts when it comes to writing.
If you want to change your slacks, you first have to
take off your shoes.

➤ Sometimes you just have to start out going in the
opposite direction to get where you really want to go.

If only writing were as easy as
good writing makes it appear.

➤ In writing, as in life, when you walk toward the light, the brightness may blind you for a time. No matter, stay the course.

You don't need to hit a **home run** with every piece of writing. A **solid base hit** will do nicely.

Write what **won't let you sleep** in the middle of the night.

TODAY AND EVERY DAY

As the quote at the beginning of this chapter reminds us, "A writer is someone who has written today." Not someone who writes for money. Not someone who writes for publication or fame. Not someone who talks about writing or reads about writing or thinks about writing or attends writers conferences. Not someone who has written in the past or will write in the future.

A writer is someone who has written today.

Writing is a **river**: You have to **keep swimming**.

> The light bulb of an idea can only go on if you have juice in the socket.

Write stories that insist on being continued beyond the last paragraph.

➤ No one has the stamina to write a book. So write a sentence, and another, and another. Sentences become paragraphs. Paragraphs become scenes. Scenes become chapters. Chapters become books. So write a sentence.

Relax, settle down in the shade of your mind.

➤ Read a first-rate short story every day. By the end of a month, your writing goals will have changed.

➤ If you write every day for a decade, you'll stand a pretty good chance of becoming an overnight success.

➤ Only a writer can know the sweet epiphany that comes of coalescing thoughts and feelings onto paper.

➤ Don't deny the world your talent.

Write to make the world something more than it is.

As the old-time lumberjacks used to say, "You gotta **keep your saw in the wood.**"

MOTIVATION:

The Excruciating
Joy of It

The fact is, it's easier to write than to want to write. Just **pick up your pen, put down a word.** Any word.

—John Dufresne, author of *Love Warps the Mind a Little*

Writing is an act of hope. It is a means of carving order from chaos, of challenging one's own beliefs and assumptions, of facing the world with eyes and heart wide open.

—Jack Heffron, author of *The Writer's Idea Book*

The writing must satisfy, must be like spoonfuls of the most delicious soup.

—Robert Olmstead, author of *Elements of the Writing Craft*

A talent is formed in stillness, a character in the stream of the world.

—Johann Wolfgang von Goethe, poet, novelist, and playwright

> **If you're writing only about yourself, you're writing only for yourself.**

➤ I don't question why I write. I question why I try to make a living at it.

➤ Many of us come to writing out of some defect ... and turn it into a strength.

WHY MY SOCKS DON'T MATCH

A poet friend, name of Jack Wonner, never wears matching socks except by coincidence. He throws his laundered socks in a drawer, unmatched. When he needs socks, he pulls out two, any two.

Hmmm. I do laundry about twenty-four times a year. Let's say I spend five minutes sorting socks. That's two hours per year. I've been doing this for forty years. That's an extra eighty hours Jack has been writing.

My socks will never match again.

We tell the world things **we did not know** until we wrote them.

The best reason to write is that **you can't *not* write.**

➤ You may hide from strong feelings in your everyday life, but not in your writing.

➤ We are at our best when we write. Not because of the talent we impose on the writing, but because of the integrity the act of writing imposes on us.

➤ Identify your greatest strength, your most troubling weakness, your most persistent fear, your most problematic issue, your most turbulent emotion. Now write.

Writing about painful subjects is less painful than **not writing** about them.

STORY STARTERS

Take a break from considering why you write and simply write.
Choose one of these openings and continue the story. Let your
motivation, whatever it may be, carry the story where it needs
to go.

His head sits on his neck like an ornamental egg in a four-point display, with the
pointy end down and thrusting forward. He wears a goatee and an earnest
expression. His features are soft-edged, as if eroded by a constant updraft. His
hair, a handful of wispy strands, is swept straight back.

A burly man of Italian descent, he often engages visitors at the tasting room of
his family winery, where he cannot talk about the wines without dancing.

Marcia, the last person in the office to realize the implications of the memo,
insisted on explaining it to me and, I suppose, to anyone else who happened to
stop by her cubicle.

Never doubt yourself, but always question **the value of your writing** for the reader.

Writing begins with a commitment that grows into a habit and **becomes a compulsion.**

> As novelist David Morrell, among others, has said, there is only one reason to write: because you have to.

We write that we may know what we are thinking.

➤ Your best writing will come of wondering and questioning, rather than of knowing and answering.

➤ It's okay to fantasize about book signings, author receptions, and award presentations. Anything that motivates your writing!

DESIRE, NOT DISCIPLINE

I used to preach that a writer must be disciplined. Seat of the pants to seat of the chair. Write every day. Blah, blah, blah. I no longer believe that.

Writing is a matter of desire, not discipline. If you want to write, that's what you'll do. If you want to write, you'll rearrange the circumstances of your life to make it possible.

If you want to write, you can't not write.

We write best what we need most to understand.

Desire is your innermost person pointing you in the direction of your natural abilities.

—Susan Meier, romance and mainstream novelist

Writing saved me from the sin and inconvenience of violence.

—Alice Walker, Pulitzer Prize-winning author of *The Color Purple*

The alchemy of fiction is, for me, an act of embalming.

—Anaïs Nin, author of *Little Birds*

If he wrote it he could get rid of it. He had gotten rid of many things by writing them.

—Ernest Hemingway, author of *A Moveable Feast*

➤ We write in order to maintain our connectedness with all things great and small—past, present, and future.

➤ Write what *others* need to have written, and you will always have a paycheck. Write what *you* need to have written, and you will always have a payoff.

Writing does not pal around with ambiguity.

➤ Write what you care about, and you will evoke emotion. Write what you know about, and you will build credibility. Write what you would like to know about, and you will discover your truth.

➤ Have fun, and your reader will too.

Write for money or write for yourself, but make up your mind.

We write to entertain and to inform. We write to assuage our ghosts. We write to earn a living. We write to create art. Mostly, we **write for the excruciating joy of it.**

THE PROCESS OF WRITING:

Writers Are Born & Then Self-Made

All good writing is swimming under water and holding your breadth.
—F. Scott Fitzgerald, author of *The Great Gatsby*

Write the truth and no one believes you: It's too alarming.
So you might as well make it up.
—Fay Weldon, author of *Wicked Women*

A well-written life is almost as rare as a well-spent one.
—Thomas Carlyle, historian and essayist

A bad book is as much of a labor to write as good a book;
it comes as sincerely from the author's soul.
—Aldous Huxley, author of *Point Counter Point*

Ideas are the easy part.

➤ When the logical mind is napping, the creative mind is ascendant. That's why you get your best ideas cleaning the garage, doing yard work, or driving across Texas.

➤ Talk about your story with friends and relatives only if you can immediately escape the conversation to write down what you just said.

> Think of your story as a movie being shown on the inside of your forehead. Tell us what the characters do and say.

Writers seek out what is familiar in the strange and what is **strange in the familiar.**

If you don't return calls from your muse, there's a chance **she'll stop calling.**

MY BEST MOMENT AS A WRITER

My best moment as a writer came when
I presented my first book to my mother.
She stood at her kitchen table with moist
eyes, repeatedly wiping the palms of her
hands on her apron before she would
touch the book.

May you know such a moment.

➤ The most important ingredient for writing well is to be well-rested. The second most important ingredient is to be off-center about something. The third most important ingredient is to be desperate.

➤ Every writer, no matter how well-published, must reinvent the confidence to write with every session.

Your memory bank is richer than you think. Just begin writing and your words will prove it.

> Don't think of it as writing in a fog of uncertainty and self-doubt. Think of it as writing in the clouds.

Writing fiction is a matter of sitting down to tell yourself a good story.

New writers **are not patient enough** with themselves.

➤ Don't worry about starting at the beginning. Just start. The beginning will reveal itself as you write.

Writing is a lot like acting, except the writer gets to play all the roles.

➤ If you talk about your story too much, your enthusiasm for it will be spent. The story will be written in the air.

➤ Do not be alarmed if your angel in the attic becomes a beast in the basement; they're the same muse.

STORY STARTERS
Having trouble starting the process of writing? Choose one of these openings and continue the story. Have fun with it. Indulge your imagination.

He did not wear the sleeveless undershirt of his father's time. Instead, he insisted on carefully pressed long-sleeved dress shirts of the heaviest fabric, hiding the coarse black hair on his chest and arms.

Marta is a sponge, an amalgamation of everyone she has ever known. She soaks up life from others. She will draw from you until you are dry.

Whenever we ate out, Gramma Ellen always ordered a grilled cheese sandwich. It wasn't until she fell and broke her hip that we discovered she had no teeth.

Make eavesdropping a way of life.

Writing is the sound of **a mind at work.** Though sometimes the sound is "clang."

➤ Ideas sing and dance in the writer's head but lurch across the page, until the writer learns to make the words sing and dance.

Write from **your wounds** and from **your triumphs.**

➤ For a multiple-choice exam, your first thought is likely to be your best bet. But not in writing.

➤ Write the first thing that comes to mind. And the second, third, and fourth. Now throw away the first three.

➤ Fool around with the order of the words until they say something better than you had in mind.

➤ Waiting in line is never a waste of time. The writer observes features, clothing, grooming, mannerisms, speech—then scribbles madly before it all runs away.

Most people regard e-mail as throwaway writing. For a writer, it's **an opportunity to practice craft.**

> Every writing
session is
practice for
the next writ-
ing session.

Write at white
heat or a slow burn.
One way or the
other, you've got to
**get the fire
in there.**

Learning by example is an elegant way of saying **copy** what works for other writers.

> It's important to write every day, thereby making yourself available for a well-written piece.

Finally, one just has to shut up, sit down, and write.

—Natalie Goldberg, author of *Writing Down the Bones*

Books choose their authors; the act of creation is not entirely a rational and conscious one.

—Salman Rushdie, author of *Midnight's Children*

To write simply is as difficult as to be good.

—W. Somerset Maugham, author of *The Razor's Edge*

We write for the same reasons we dream—because we cannot not dream, because it is the nature of the human imagination to dream.

—Joyce Carol Oates, author *I Am No One You Know: Stories*

DON'T WAIT

If you wait for inspiration, it may only come every fifteen years, even if it is prize-winning inspiration. Better to adopt the mantra favored by most working writers: butt-in-chair, hands-on-keyboard.

➤ If you're excited about writing a future scene, by all means write it. Don't worry about writing scenes in sequence.

➤ As with most worthwhile endeavors, those outside writing will see the outcome, but not the process.

If you set a piece aside to breathe for a while, be sure to return to it before it molds.

Writing a first novel **is like getting reacquainted** with the person you never were.

➤ Whatever you are writing, writing will change it. Whoever you are, writing will change you.

➤ Every piece of writing is an approximation. With each rewrite, you will glean something of use in the final draft, or at least eliminate another lousy approximation.

Given the opportunity, a writer will **fiddle** with a piece of writing **forever.**

The short story is intended to be received **in one sitting:** the reader's, **not the writer's.**

> The written expression of a painful experience contains the experience, makes it manageable and tolerable, and opens the writer to healing.

➤ When you finish a piece of writing, you own the writing, you own the process, and you own a piece of yourself.

➤ If you finish a piece of writing in a single draft, you're exceptionally talented at either writing or self-deception.

The writing is **always lousy** until it's not. **Then it's finished.**

A person may be born with
the potential to be a writer,
**but every writer
is self-made.**

WRITER'S BLOCK:

Write About Your Secret Life

Writer's block is a fancy term made up by whiners **so they can have an excuse to drink alcohol.**

—Steve Martin, author and actor

There is nothing to write about, you say. Well then, write and let me know just this—that there is nothing to write about.

—Pliny the Younger, Roman author

Writing a book is a horrible, exhausting struggle, like a long bout of some painful illness. One would never undertake such a thing if one were not driven on by some demon whom one can neither resist nor understand.

—George Orwell, author of *Animal Farm* and *1984*

➤ Nature abhors a vacuum and will immediately fill it with whatever is at hand. The blank page is a vacuum and you are Mother Nature.

Nowhere in a book contract does it say, **"If you feel like it."**

Writing is the **only known cure** for not writing.

➤ Writer's block does not spring upon one full-blown; it worms its way into your consciousness. Dispel the first and every subsequent wiggling doubt.

➤ Writer's block is rooted in self-doubt. Forget others. Write for your eyes only.

A negative attitude will **erode your creative landscape** more surely than a torrent of criticism.

➤ Approach each writing session with curiosity and a kind of dreamlike anticipation. In short, recapture the approach to life you had as a child.

➤ Create an ideal reader in your mind. Picture your reader in detail, attentive and friendly, interested and intelligent. Now tell your reader a story.

Writers make sentences.
Wanna-bes make excuses.

KITCHEN TIMER

If you have a desire to write, but can't quite get to it, set your kitchen timer for fifteen minutes. You can do *anything* for fifteen minutes. Early on in these writing sessions, allow yourself to quit when you hear the timer ring. As your writing habit develops, you'll learn to ignore the bell. Before long, you won't need to set the timer. You'll simply sit down, open a vein, and write until you're spent. One day you'll come up for air from a writing session to find you've been at it for a couple of hours. Then you'll need to start setting the kitchen timer to remind you of when it's time to pick up the kids.

Your work will not be judged by your first draft. **No one need see it but you.**

➤ It's all right to allow an idea to percolate for a while. It's not all right to excuse yourself from putting the idea on paper.

There is no penalty for lousy first drafts.

➤ Sit down. Write a sentence. Now write another sentence. Write as many as you need to until the good stuff comes.

➤ The first three or four pages of writing are often a warm-up, but you still have to work through them to get to the good stuff.

It is better to write poorly than to not write at all.

➤ If for a time you can't write well, write poorly. You can fix it later or throw it away.

➤ Give some airtime to the critics in your head, if you must, then tell them to shut up and listen while you write.

STORY STARTERS

Smash through writer's block! Choose one of these openings and continue the story. Make it your own.

Lydia named all the critters who bounded around and under her bungalow. This latest, which she believed to be either a marten or a ferret, she named George, after the whiskered man from the co-op who read her electric meter every other month.

Jason placed a dab of shaving cream just below his right ear and headed for the mall. Today he would again linger outside the plus-size shop. Surely the same woman would not appear and wipe away the shaving cream two days in a row. He preferred a new adventure.

Franklin wears the same size pants he did as a teenager, though at a different angle. And he still hitches his waistband when he sees a girl he might like to kiss, as he did now.

You needn't be **in control of your material** to begin writing—only to finish.

> Start with whatever part of the story you most want to write and write as much as you can about it. Write forward and backward from your starting point.

➤ Don't fret much about your story's title, or let that keep you from starting. The title is the item most often changed by editors.

Write down **the first three ideas** that come to mind, but don't promise to use any of them.

Write quickly, open the door to your subconscious before your internal editor **can take control.**

➤ Start with whatever you have: a scene, a snatch of dialogue, a character's mannerism. You can fill in the details and sort them all out later.

If they're meant to be writers, they will write. **There's nothing that can stop them.**
—Tennessee Williams, playwright

Think of it not as writer's block but as writer's search.
—Gordon Lish, author of *What I Know So Far: Stories*

Great things are not accomplished by those who yield to trends and fads and popular opinion.
—Charles Kuralt, broadcast journalist and author

Every writer I know has trouble writing.
—Joseph Heller, author of *Catch-22* and *Something Happened*

➤ Work on more than one piece of writing at a time. When one stalls, move to another.

➤ Write about an everyday incident from a different point of view, e.g., an SUV runs off a country road and crashes into a haybale—written from the haybale's point of view.

Write a cover blurb for your story—as if it were being published as a mass market paperback.

Write a story **about pluck.** Of individual courage and initiative and effort **rewarded.**

If you're stuck, **write a letter to a friend** explaining what you're trying to write.

➤ Reading, meditation, a new environment, music, art, exercise, rest, sex, food, or beverage: Any of these may stimulate your creativity. Find out what works for you.

➤ If you get stuck, remember this: Libraries and bookstores are chock full of the greatest writing teachers in the world.

➤ Add to your resource files: bits of dialogue that catch your ear, clothes or signs or business names that catch your eye, incidents in the grocery store, mannerisms of everyday people, apt phrases, "what-if" questions ...

Consider what you would most like to do **if you dared.** Now do it **through your characters.**

NO SUCH THING AS CASUAL WRITING

Everything you write is an opportunity to practice your craft, whether it's a sympathy note, a personal letter, an e-mail message, or an anecdote in your journal. Express yourself as well as you can at that particular moment. Don't settle for bits and pieces. Don't tell yourself this doesn't count as real writing. Good writing is a habit. Rewrite everything. Make every piece of writing the best it can be.

Write the part of the story you wouldn't show your mother.

➤ Keep an "asylum file" for all your crazy ideas. Check the file from time to time to see which of the inmates have begun to make sense.

➤ When you finish a writing session, leave off with a specific question to be answered in the next scene or section, or write a one-sentence summary of what happens next.

Watch music videos. They will stimulate your mind to indulge in **weird connections.**

➤ If you worry about what your mother will think when she reads your work, your mother will likely be the only one to ever read it.

➤ If you find it difficult to make something up, you're probably trying too hard. Instead, record the details of everyday life as you know it—and exaggerate.

➤ Stash unfinished stories in a "ripening file." Use an actual brown paper bag. Throw in a banana, if you like. Check the bag for newly ripened stories every few days.

Write about **what's inside of you.** What makes you angry, tearful, joyful, peaceful?

Write about **your secret life.** The one you live in your head.

THE WRITING LIFE:

Everything Speaks
to a Writer

The best time for planning a book is while you're doing the dishes.

—Agatha Christie, detective novelist and playwright

I walk my dogs in the morning and map out what I'm going to do that day in my head. Then I go home and do it. Very boring process, really.

—Dennis Lehane, author of *Mystic River*

You write until you come to a place where you still have your juice and know what will happen next and you stop and try to live through until the next day when you hit it again.

—Ernest Hemingway, author of *Old Man and the Sea*

To make writing a priority, one must give up something else.

➤ You can peek behind the refrigerator, search the attic, rattle through the junk drawer. You won't find time for writing.

➤ To find yourself as a writer, you'll likely look in all the wrong places, then find yourself close to home.

If you write every day, about once a month writing will be a picnic with polite ants.

➤ Writing is more than an occupation, more than a profession. Writing is an identity.

➤ Not only must you renew your commitment to writing every day, you must work up your nerve again and again.

Write every day. It's the best way to treat your neuroses.

Writers have friends, to be sure, but **mostly writers have sources.**

> If you are concerned that your writing may wound a friend or relative, keep writing. You are writing from the heart.

➤ As writers, we discover truths about ourselves and others, only to forget them. And then, happily or not, we rediscover them.

➤ Understand life as well as you can, so that your readers might live with understanding as well as they can.

In writing, as in life, **people want you to be honest**—until you say things they don't want to hear.

THE CAT IN THE HAT

Most writers are at the same time incredibly insecure and unconscionably confident. Who else but a writer would type a bunch of squiggly marks on paper and expect other people to pay for the privilege of looking at them.

In the Spring of 2000, a bookstore in Erie, Pennsylvania, invited me speak in conjunction with a nationwide essay contest. When I arrived, the parking lot was jammed. There were two television vans! "Whoa, this is a much bigger deal than I expected," I thought. So I straightened my tie, puffed myself up, and strode into the store.

About twenty chairs were arranged classroom style for my presentation ... with nary a soul in sight. I struggled through my presentation with only a handful of participants. Where was everybody?

Finally, I heard a commotion at the other end of the store. Parents and kids (and television crews) were clustered around The Cat in the Hat, who was appearing the same afternoon. I had been upstaged by a high school kid in a cat costume.

Just about the time you are feeling your oats as a writer, something will happen to bring you back to the barn.

Writing fosters the illusion that you can actually gain control over your life.

➤ Write in order to make sense out of some aspect of your life, and you will likely do the same for your readers.

➤ The lower levels of your consciousness are far more honest than the upper levels. Trust your instincts.

➤ A writer is never off duty.

➤ Many published writers fear they are not real writers, that they will be discovered to be frauds. Or that they will never be able to do it again. Just like you and me.

➤ At some point you will consider yourself more talented and productive than the people around you. This is a terrible situation for a writer.

A fair number of fiction writers **have been avid liars since childhood.**

➤ Every writer endures this basic paradox: Whatever you write is wholly original (a result of your particular experiences, attitudes, knowledge, and style) and wholly unoriginal (been done before, been said before, been written before).

➤ The most enduring relationship a writer will have in this world is with writing.

A writer may leave off writing for a time. A writer **cannot leave off being a writer.**

Writers are cannibals. ... It is a terrible thing to be the friend, the acquaintance, the relative of a writer.

—Cynthia Ozick, novelist and short-story writer

If I understood half of what I did or what I felt, I probably wouldn't waste my time writing. But I like the probing.

—Terry McMillan, author of *A Day Late and a Dollar Short*

The writer's own responsibility is to his art. He will be completely ruthless if he is a good one. He has a dream. It anguishes him so much he must get rid of it.

—William Faulkner, Nobel Prize-winning author

Every good writer is a sponge: soak it up, wring it out.

➤ Whoever said, "No news is good news," was not a writer.

➤ For a writer, no experience is complete until it's written down.

➤ Being a writer has two main advantages and both of them are freedom.

> Nothing bad ever happens to a writer; it's all grist for the mill.

Trouble comes regularly to a writer's household. And it's always welcome.

Writing is a great way of life and a lousy way to make a living.

➤ As with acting, writing offers consummate freedom, allowing exploration of the self under the guise of character.

➤ For many writers, writing is the most fun they can have doing something for which they might get paid.

Better a literary career ruined by the pursuit of life than the other way around.

➤ For a writer, school is never out. Every time you sit down to write, it's a take-home exam.

➤ What you wrote a year ago or a month ago or yesterday is now another writer's work.

No one ever masters writing, though a few get closer than most.

> Thank those who help you learn to write, of course—and those who let you.

To be a writer, you must sentence yourself to **a life of solitary refinement.**

Every writer spends a lifetime as **a writer-in-training.**

➤ As we grow older, we continually reinvent our lives. Writers pause to apply for copyrights along the way.

Unlike many skills, writing often improves with age.

➤ As to writing as a career, if you can take it or leave it, leave it.

➤ To experience burnout as a writer, you must first be on fire.

STORY STARTERS
Even everyday events touch a writer. Choose one of these openings, and continue the story.

Ronnie stood at the bottom of the up escalator, his tongue plastered against the handrail. "Thee, I ken lick ta whole fing wiffout moving." His buddy Lonnie looked around for something he could do.

Phillip felt obliged to seek out opportunities for political incorrectness. To him, cultural mores were an outgrowth of posturing rather than principle. His principles led him to barge into the book discussion group at Barnes & Noble, armed with wasp repellent and Kwik-Glue.

Even with the football game on TV, I could hear my sister-in-law giggling upstairs in the kitchen. What could she find so entertaining about Slim Zippy, the deacon who brought Gram communion every Sunday. She laughed again. This time her gaiety seemed forced. My brother, Tim, stopped his beer in mid-air and cocked his head toward the stairwell.

➤ Creativity is an undisciplined rascal, always wanting to move on to the next thing, never quite finishing the project at hand.

Stand in the rain with your face turned upward every chance you get.

Your favorite piece of writing will always be **your next one.**

Every writer has **a lot of unfinished stuff,** including a lot of the published stuff.

➤ Writing is sometimes like studying. You sit there almost comatose, and, while nothing appears to be happening, all hell is breaking loose in your head.

➤ Cranking your engine when you're out of gas will only run down your battery. Learn to accept that sometimes you need to refuel.

Writing is mostly thinking,
sometimes on paper.

> Just as a doctor engages in the practice of medicine, a writer engages in the practice of writing, only for a lot less money.

> As a writer, all the people you meet will expect you to have read everything they've ever read.

Writers spend a lot of time finding out what they can't do, only to discover **they can do it.**

➤ You came to writing because of the person you are. In time, you will become the person you are because of the writing.

➤ Police officers need to be observant. Writers need to be absorbent.

Writing allows you to achieve **a level of personal integrity** to which you can only aspire in real life.

> **Writing is a private act and a public trust.**

> **For a writer, "nothing" never happens.**

A writer works **alone** and must, therefore, suffer **the company of a fool.**

The creative muse is nothing more than a nag, and **a possessive nag** at that.

Writing is a jealous mistress.

➤ If you have the talent, attitude, and opportunity to write well, you are blessed beyond measure and ought not to ask for anything more.

➤ Some writers compete with other writers. Better writers compete with themselves. The best writers compete with the possible.

It isn't necessary that a writer's experience be wide, **only that it be deep.**

➤ If you haven't gone anywhere without paper and pencil in the past year, you're a writer.

> When immersed in a river of success, a writer must learn to breathe underwater.

Writers are of necessity **self-reliant.** Not to be confused with self-sufficient.

➤ Never talk about a story idea at a party. Either you'll spend your enthusiasm for the story, or you'll have to leave the party to write it.

➤ Friends and relatives perceive a writing life to mean you are always available and in need of a break, or you are never available and should not be disturbed.

What other enterprise offers you the opportunity to speak from beyond the grave?

Everything
speaks to a writer.

CRITICS AND CRITIQUES:

Punch a Critter in the Nose

Asking a working writer how he **feels about critics** is like asking a lamppost how it **feels about dogs.**

—Christopher Hampton, playwright

There's only one person a writer should listen to, pay any attention to. It's not any damn critic. It's the reader.

—William Styron, Pulitzer Prize-winning author

It's easier to write about those you hate—just as it's easier to criticize a bad play or a bad book.

—Dorothy Parker, short-story writer and poet

Nature, when she invented, manufactured, and patented her authors, contrived to make critics out of the chips that were left.

—Oliver Wendell Holmes, Sr., poet and humorist

Those who love you often make excellent first readers—**for someone else's writing.**

➤ We all need our early readers—friends and relatives who wade through our drafts and tell us it's wonderful. And, if we're lucky, some of our early readers will tell us when it isn't so wonderful.

➤ When early readers ask why you wrote a certain way, put off explaining until you find out how it affected them.

Treat early readers with the same **respect and courtesy** as you would a professional editor.

Seek out the opinions of **readers of integrity** and your writing will reflect the same.

STAN THE LOGGER

One of my early readers is a logger who goes to bed butt-tired every night. Stan often falls asleep reading one of my stories, wrinkling the pages he hasn't read yet. When Stan returns a story to me I always listen carefully to his comments, but I pay most attention to the wrinkled pages. I rewrite the passages leading up to those pages. One of my goals is to write a story that will keep Stan awake all the way through.

➤ Heaven bless the critters: early readers who offer heartfelt—and sometimes appropriate—suggestions to improve our writing.

➤ Bless those who show you what's weak in your writing. Twice bless those who teach you to see what's weak in your writing.

All we can hope to offer, all we can hope to receive, is an honest critique.

> **Every writer needs others to point out weaknesses he or she would readily recognize in someone else's writing.**

If you allow only admirers to read your work, **they will probably admire it.**

STORY STARTERS

Forget the critics, especially the critics in your head. Choose one of these openings, and let the story roll.

The hard candies, each wrapped in cellophane, looked undersized and out of place in the palm of his hand. A workingman's hand. She selected the only variety of candy of which there were two. He selected the other.

Tim chose the best of my sweaters to wear for the day. Had the situation been reversed, I would have borrowed the least of the lot. We are brothers in a thousand ways, and in a thousand ways not.

My sister has the listening skills of a blow dryer. Talking with her is like talking to a flat tire. She fills the air with gibberish until my ears grow hoarse. That is, she did until her automobile accident, which will happen in eleven days.

Focus on identifying
what is wrong,
not on how to fix it.
Fixing comes
later.

The point is not whether a piece of writing breaks a rule, but whether **it is effective.**

➤ The first step toward publication is moving from submitting your work for praise to submitting your work for critique.

If you receive similar comments from several early readers, **pay attention.**

➤ When your early readers say a character isn't interesting, that they just didn't care about the character, take it to heart.

➤ If more than one reader tells you he or she had to reread a passage to understand it, rewrite the passage.

Any authentic work of art must **start an argument** between the artist and his audience.

—Rebecca West, author of *The Return of the Soldier*

If you can honestly say you've done your best, your work has already passed the only test that matters.

—Marshall J. Cook, coauthor of *Give 'Em What They Want: How to Successfully Pitch Your Novel*

It's very, very destructive to judge yourself. It's much more instructive to observe yourself.

—Jane Smiley, author of *A Thousand Acres*

If it can't be read aloud, it's no good.

—John Braine, author of *How to Write a Novel* and *Room at the Top*

➤ Critics are mosquitoes and you are a pony with no tail. But you *are* a pony and they are mosquitoes.

A critique group **might fix your story** the way a veterinarian fixes a dog.

➤ Critique groups tend to push all work toward the middle. Caution: There isn't any cutting edge in the middle.

➤ Respect the opinions of others, but ultimately trust yourself to judge what is right for your work.

Practice may improve your writing. **Examined practice** will *surely* improve your writing.

A thoughtful critique provides the writer with an opportunity to improve the work and, metaphorically, punch a critter in the nose.

FOR NEW WRITERS ONLY:
If You Can Dream It

> However great a man's natural talent may be, the art of writing **cannot be learned all at once.**
>
> —Jean-Jacques Rousseau, author and philosopher

> No one can really tell a beginning writer whether or not he has what it takes. ... The young writer must decide for himself, on the available evidence.
>
> —John Gardner, author of *On Becoming a Novelist*

> I was a writing fool when I was eleven years old and have been tapering off ever since.
>
> —E.B. White, author of *Charlotte's Web* and *Stuart Little*

> Most of the basic material a writer works with is acquired before the age of fifteen.
>
> —Willa Cather, Pulitzer Prize-winning author of *One of Ours*

You don't have to write the beginning first.

> If you're a new writer, you have many advantages over more seasoned writers. You don't have to live up to what you've done before, you feel everything keenly, and you are wildly enthusiastic.

➤ Writing is a process of discovery. You will discover the story as you write.

➤ Start with whatever comes to mind: an action scene, an unusual character, a puzzle to be solved, a bit of conversation, a description of a particular place.

You don't have to know **the whole story** before you begin writing.

NEVER AGAIN

You will never again be quite the person you are today.

While it is true that your writing will improve with practice, especially examined practice, what you write today is not merely practice. Right now, you are feeling certain emotions as keenly as you will ever feel them in your life. These emotions, as well as your experiences and understandings of the world, are worth writing about.

What you write today is important and valid.

> You don't have to make it perfect on the first try. You don't even have to make it good on the first try or the second try. Or even on the third try.

Working writers hardly ever write well **on the first try.** It usually takes many rewrites to write well. Even for famous writers.

The best thing about writing? There is **no wrong way to do it.**

➤ Sometimes we have to write our way through the crummy stuff to get to the good stuff.

➤ You don't have to live an exciting life or travel to faraway places to be a writer. Instead, create a character readers care about.

To be a writer, you **don't have to know** a lot of big words or fancy techniques.

Suppose you could **read the mind** of someone you meet. Tell us what he or she is thinking and feeling.

➤ Write about a person you met in a book who reminds you of a person you know in real life.

STORY STARTERS
You can tell your stories any way you like. Choose one of these openings and show us what happens next.

Fatigue settled over the bus driver like silent snow, still a good two hundred miles east of Albuquerque. Most of the passengers dozed, but Nate Desmond absorbed the night sky and shadowed buttes, in no hurry to see his wife and children.

It isn't simply that she's wide-eyed. She has an expectant look in her eyes, the lilt of curiosity in her voice, as if something unexpected and wondrous is about to happen, as if the very next moment of her life is sure to be the best ever. It is this endearing quality that led to the old man's murder.

Five years old and as absorbent as a terry cloth towel, my granddaughter, Kiki, watches the flickering cartoon characters. They at least speak to her.

If someone reads your story and says, **"I could have written that,"** you are a terrific writer.

➤ Usually we write about what we see or hear. Try writing about how something smells, how something tastes, how something feels on your skin.

➤ Ask yourself, "What is the best thing that could happen next?" "What is the worst thing that could happen next?" You get to choose!

Include just enough details, usually about three, so the reader can **visualize each scene.**

Good writing always reads as if it **were easy to do.** That's what makes it good writing.

➤ You can't be there to explain what your readers should be feeling, so make sure they feel it on the page.

> If I had to give young writers advice, I'd say **don't listen to writers talking about writing.**
> —Lillian Hellman, playwright

One needs inspiration to write when one is twenty. At the age of sixty, there's the mess of one's entire life and little time remaining to worry.
—Charles Simic, Pulitzer Prize-winning poet

The beautiful part of writing is that you don't have to get it right the first time, unlike, say, a brain surgeon.
—Robert Cormier, author of *After the First Death*

The trade of authorship is a violent and indestructible obsession.
—George Sand, novelist and playwright

➤ You'll labor over your first story. And, in the end, it may not amount to much. Not to worry: It will make you want to write another one.

➤ What somebody else wants you to write is hardly ever what you want to write.

We first learn to write by reading. It pretty much stays that way over the course of a lifetime.

If you can
dream it, you
can write it.

ABOUT THE AUTHOR

Paul Raymond Martin has published more than three hundred stories, poems, and articles. He is the author of *Writer's Little Instruction Book: Inspiration & Motivation*, *Writer's Little Instruction Book: Craft & Technique*, and *Writer's Little Instruction Book: Getting Published*, all from Writer's Digest Books.

Paul lives on a seventy-acre farm in northwestern Pennsylvania, where he leases the fields to a neighboring farmer. When he's not writing, Paul likes to play in the dirt and raise wormy apples.